MEASURING UP!

EXPERIMENTS, PUZZLES, AND GAMES EXPLORING MEASUREMENT

Measuring Up!

EXPERIMENTS, PUZZLES, AND GAMES EXPLORING MEASUREMENT

Sandra Markle

Atheneum Books for Young Readers

F*or Betty Alge for being special in all those
ways that can never be measured.*

The author would especially like to thank *Merri L. Schroeder, Dr. Deborah Ball*
of Michigan State University, and *Dr. Gerald H. Krockover* of Perdue University,
for sharing their expertise and enthusiasm.

On the recommendation of the expert consultants, some of the measuring activities in this
book use the imperial scale, while others use the metric scale. Readers are encouraged to
think in one scale or the other rather than to make conversions, which could be confusing.
The activities have been devised under the curriculum standards developed by the National
Council of Teachers of Mathematics.

Atheneum Books for Young Readers
An imprint of Simon & Schuster Children's Publishing Division
1230 Avenue of the Americas
New York, NY 10020

Book design by Anne Scatto/PIXEL PRESS

The text of this book is set in Monotype Horley Old Style.

First edition

Manufactured in the United States of America
10 9 8 7 6 5 4 3 2 1

Library of Congress Cataloging-in-Publication Data

Markle, Sandra.
Measuring up!: experiments, puzzles, and games
exploring measurement / by Sandra Markle. — 1st ed.
p. cm.
ISBN 0-689-31904-5
1. Physical measurements—Juvenile literature. 2. Physical measurements—
Experiments—Juvenile literature. [1. Physical measurements—Experiments.
2. Experiments. 3. Scientific recreations.] I. Title
QC39.M365   1995   94-19240
520.8—dc20   CIP   AC

PHOTO CREDITS: *Cover* Rob McDonald; *title page* Rob McDonald; *pages 1-3* Rob McDonald; *page 3* Manute Bol; *pages 4-5* Dennis J. Schotzko, University of Idaho; *page 6* William Markle, CompuART; *pages 7-8* Rob McDonald; *page 10* William Markle, CompuART; *page 11* Manute Bol; *page 12* Atlanta Braves; *page 13* William Markle, CompuART; *page 14* Rawlings Sporting Goods Company; *page 15* National Portrait Gallery, Smithsonian Institution/Art Resource, NY; *page 16* U.S. Forest Service; *page 18* Rob McDonald; *pages 19-21* William Markle, CompuART; *pages 23-24* Rob McDonald; *page 25* William Markle, CompuART; *page 26* Rob McDonald; *pages 28-29* William Markle, CompuART; *page 30* Atlanta Falcons; *page 31* William Markle, CompuART; *page 33* Rob McDonald; *page 35* Charleston Tea Plantation, Inc.; *pages 38-41* William Markle, CompuART.

CONTENTS

Getting Started

- What if Manute Bol, the tallest player in the National Basketball Association, was planning to spend the weekend with you. Could he sleep in one of your family's beds without his feet hanging over the end?

- Ever wonder how much heavier a football player is once he puts on all his gear?

- Wish you could figure out if a large soft drink is really a better buy than the small size?

- Want to make an instrument that will let you measure something really tall, like a big tree or your house?

- Want to make a tool you can use to easily measure how far you have to walk to the bus stop or to a friend's house?

This book will let you do all this and more!

You'll make a balance scale and use it to make a crafty mobile. You'll measure out the ingredients to whip up your own fortune cookies, and check the temperature as you bake up a batch of pretzels. You'll take a look inside a baseball and test its bounce, set up a treasure hunt that's fun for you to construct and for your friends to follow. You'll perform an experiment that lets you measure which toilet tissue is the sturdiest. And you'll find lots of games and puzzles to keep you thinking and measuring.

You may be surprised to discover just how many different ways measuring skills are useful. You definitely won't want to miss any of the measuring fun!

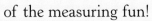

MEASURING SIZES AND DISTANCES

CHECKERED BEETLE (*Enoclerus eximius*)

WILD BUGS

You may never have seen insects quite like these even though they were photographed in Idaho and Washington. They're shown here much bigger than life so you can get a better look.

To find out how big each really is, measure the line below each insect. Use the Imperial scale to record measurements in inches. Now find something at home that is just as long as the pink cricket; as short as the checkered bettle.

Check yourself on page 42.

STRAWBERRY CLEARWING MOTH (*Hemaris diffinis*)

CUCKOO WASP (*Chrysis* sp.)

For more fun, start your own insect collection. For information on how to do this, write to: Young Entomologists' Society (1915 Peggy Place, Lansing, Michigan 48910-2553). Be sure to measure all the insects you include in your collection.

PINK CRICKET (*Steiroxys* sp.)

TEXAS BEETLE LARVA (*Brachypsectra fulva*)

EYE TRICKS

These are called optical illusions because what you see isn't necessarily what's real. First guess the measurement in each of these optical illusions. Use a ruler to find out if you were fooled. Then see if these optical illusions will trick a friend. Check the solutions on page 42.

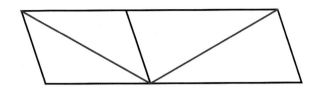

* Which line is longer, the red line or the blue line?

* Which is greater, the height of the hat or the width of its hat brim?

* Which center circle is bigger—the red one or the blue one?

Here's an optical illusion you can make to fool your eyes and trick a friend. Cut in about three inches toward the center of a paper plate. Cut halfway around the plate; then snip back to the rim, cutting out a paper arch. Next, bring the ends of this arch together and crease. Cut along the fold line.

Place one half of the arch above the other. Then ask a friend to indicate which one is longer or whether they are the same length. Does one half arch now look longer to you?

To prove to yourself and your friend that the lengths of the arches are identical, lay one on top of the other. Or measure the distance along the upper edge of each arch. Your eyes were fooled because you were comparing the longer side of the bottom arch to the shorter side of the top arch.

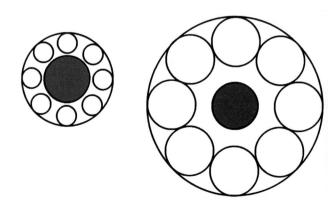

MAKE A CLINOMETER

Want to know how tall a flagpole is? Or maybe you'd like to check how well you guessed the height of a really big tree? A clinometer will let you measure these tall objects.

You'll need:

- a protractor (plastic protractors are available at office supply stores and some grocery stores)
- 20 centimeters of string
- steel washer
- clear packaging tape
- plastic straw

Tie one end of the string to the steel washer. Place the free end of the string across the center line of the protractor and secure it with a piece of tape on the straight edge. Also tape the straw so it's lying along the straight edge of the protractor.

To use the clinometer, look through the straw at the tip-top of the object you want to measure. Backing up slowly, stop when the string stretches across the forty-five-degree mark on the protractor. A partner can help you.

Now, stand still while your partner measures from your feet to the base of the object to be measured. If it's a fairly long distance, you'll want to use the hodometer you'll be making next. Also have your partner measure the distance from your feet to your eyes. Add these two measurements together to discover the approximate height of the object being measured.

Try It Out

Use your clinometer to find the height of each of these objects. Just for fun, estimate each object's height first. Then measure to check yourself.

1. A streetlamp
2. A house at its highest point
3. A billboard
4. A flagpole
5. A wall (inside a house or building)

MAKE A HODOMETER

Now, here's a tool that will let you measure distances too long to measure easily with a ruler or tape measure. It's called a hodometer.

To make a hodometer that measures distances in meters, you'll need:

pencil

20 centimeters of string

tape measure showing the metric scale

scissors

2 squares of sturdy corrugated
    cardboard 35 centimeters across

white glue

yardstick or any meter-long sturdy,
    thin piece of flat wood for the handle

2.5-centimeter-long screw with
    a sharp tip

duct tape

3 old magazines

2 metal washers

permanent marker

safety goggles

NOTE: *You may want to have an adult partner work with you.*

First, make a dot in the center of one cardboard square. You can find the center by stretching the string across the cardboard from opposite corners and drawing along this line. Then stretch the string across the other set of opposite corners and draw along this line. Draw an "X" at the point where the two lines cross in the center.

    Tie one end of the string near the pencil's point. Measure out 15.7 centimeters (or just a tiny bit less than 16 centimeters). Place that point on the string at the center of the cardboard. Keep the string taut while you move the pencil around the center dot, drawing a circle. Cut out the circle and use it as a pattern to cut out a second circle. Coat one circle with glue and press the two circles together with the corrugated lines crisscrossing for strength. Let dry for about thirty minutes.

Put on your safety goggles. Place the cardboard circles on the stack of magazines. Slowly turn the screw into the cardboard circles at the center dot until it goes through. Turn the screw in the opposite direction to remove it. Place the yardstick on the magazines. Make a mark 7.5 centimeters from one end. Twist the screw into the wood until it goes all the way through this mark. Twist the screw back out again. Next, thread one washer onto the screw, put the screw through the cardboard circles, thread on the second washer, and twist the screw into the hole in the yardstick. If the wheel doesn't turn easily, loosen the screw. Wrap the pointed end of the screw with tape.

Draw an arrow aimed at any point on the outside edge of the wheel. To measure distances in meters, hold the hodometer with the arrow pointing at the ground and walk slowly, rolling the wheel across the ground. Every time the arrow returns to its starting position, you've walked one meter. To measure distances of less than a meter, place the zero end of the tape measure at the arrow and wrap it around the outer rim of the hodometer's wheel. Make a mark every ten centimeters on the wheel. Then you can measure how far you've gone in meters and decimeters (ten centimeters is equal to one decimeter).

NOTE: *If you want to make a hodometer that measures yards instead of meters, draw the circle with a string 5 3/4 inches long (or just a little less than 6 inches).*

Try It Out

Here are some opportunities to try out your hodometer:

1. Measure the distance around the sides of your room.

2. Find out how far it is from your room to your family's front door.

3. Go outdoors. Pick out an object, such as a tree or lamp post, and estimate how many meters away it is. Check yourself.

4. How far can you walk in one minute? Take a guess. Then find out.

5. An alligator may grow to be about five meters long. Use objects to mark the starting and stopping point for a distance you think is as long as an alligator. Use the hodometer to check your estimate.

TRACKING DOWN TREASURE

Nothing is more fun than a treasure hunt. So set one up for your friends and then invite them to join you for a treasure-hunting party.

First, you'll need a starting point, such as a tree or bush. Use a compass to set the direction you'll have your friends head as they set off on the first leg of the hunt. If you are not familiar with how to use a compass, check with an adult who knows and practice before you begin. Next, use the hodometer to measure the distance your friends will travel in that direction. Write the direction and distance to travel on a piece of paper that can be given out at the beginning of the treasure hunt. Remember that your friends will need a compass and hodometer in order to follow your directions.

Next, choose a new direction for your friends to head during the second leg of the hunt and measure off the distance they will need to travel this time. Plant a note with the new travel directions where it can be easily found at the end of the first leg. Each leg of the hunt will need to end with a new set of travel directions. Be sure to check that each leg of the hunt is free of any obstacles. Six to eight legs is a good length for a treasure hunt. At the very end, leave goodies, such as apples or oranges, in a box decorated to look like a treasure chest.

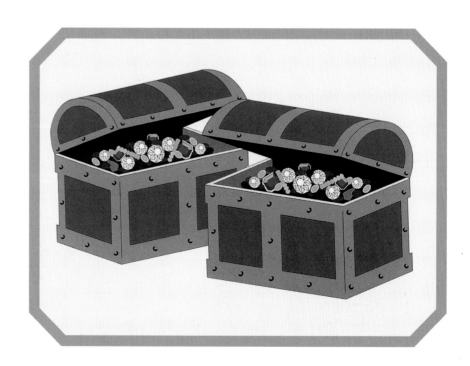

MANUTE SLEPT HERE

Manute Bol, at seven feet seven inches tall, is the tallest person ever to play in the National Basketball Association (NBA), and he's coming to spend the weekend with *you*. It's going to be great to have him visit, but where will he sleep?

Listed below are the lengths and diagonal distances across a standard twin-, full-, queen-, and king-size bed. Predict how much of Manute will hang off the end if he sleeps straight or stretches diagonally across each bed. Then find out how well you guessed by computing how much of Manute really will hang over if he sleeps in each of these beds. Check yourself by looking on page 42.

BEDS	LENGTH	DIAGONAL
Twin	74 inches	81 inches
Full	74 inches	88 inches
Queen	78 inches	96 inches
King	78 inches	108 inches

Suppose the only bed you have to offer Manute is twin-size. Is there anything you could do to help Manute sleep comfortably? Maybe hook up a hammock to the ceiling for his feet? Brainstorm—you'll come up with lots more ideas. List all you can think of in one minute. Which do you think is best?

RUNNING HOME

Here's Henry (Hank) Aaron driving in his 700th home run. He went on to hit a record 755 home runs before he retired in 1974.

Who ran more yards for his record, though, Hank Aaron or Walter Payton? Aaron circled the bases for his 755 home runs. Payton earned his running record on the football field where he covered 16,726 yards for the National Football League career record for most yards gained rushing (According to the *Guinness Book of Word Records,* 1994 Edition.)

To solve this problem, start by writing what steps you'll need to take and what operations you'll need to perform. You probably already guessed that first you'll have to find out how many yards Aaron ran circling the bases once. It's 90 feet (30 yards) between each base. Check yourself by looking on page 42.

Now, here's more baseball fun. The longest throw using the current baseball was 445 feet 10 inches by Glen Gorbous on August 20, 1974. If you stood just outside the front door of your house or apartment building and threw a ball as far as Glen Gorbous did, where would it probably land? You may want to use the hodometer you made to find out, but check with an adult first to be sure it will be safe for you to measure. Since the hodometer measures in meters, you'll need to know that 445 feet 10 inches is about 135 meters.

TOP BOUNCER

Ever think about why a ball bounces? The material it's made out of is compressed to some degree when it strikes the ground, a bat, or a wall. As the material returns to its original shape, the ball rebounds. That rebound is a bounce. Do some balls have more bounce than others? Here's a bounce test you can use to find out. Do this with a friend.

You'll need a yard stick and at least five different kinds of balls, such as a tennis ball, a golf ball, a baseball, a volleyball, and a soccer ball. The more balls you test the better, so you may have to borrow some from friends. Predict which type of ball you think will bounce best. Then test your prediction.

Set up a test site outdoors on a smooth flat sidewalk or playground. Hold your arm straight out in front of you. When you drop a ball, have your friend put a hand out to mark how high the ball jumps up on its first bounce. Measure the distance from the ground to your friend's hand and record the bounce height. Test each ball's bounce three times to make sure a result you get isn't just a freak occurrence. Next, add up the totals for each ball and divide by three to find the average height each ball bounced.

Did one ball have more bounce than another? Make a list of all the reasons why one ball might rebound better than another. For example, could the ball's size affect its bounce? Or is there any irregularity, such as a protruding piece of lacing, that could have affected its bounce? You'll probably think of lots of other possibilities.

You may be interested to learn how the Rawlings Sporting Goods Company, supplier of baseballs to the major leagues, tests how well its baseballs bounce. One ball selected at random from each lot produced is shot out of an air cannon at 80 miles per hour. It's aimed at a wall about ten feet away that's made of ash, the same kind of wood used for most wooden bats. Special instruments time the speed at which the ball bounces away from the wall to make sure it's lively enough but not too lively. That way it's a player's skill and not the ball that makes the difference in a game's outcome.

GAME CALLED ON ACCOUNT OF COLD

Should baseball games be canceled if the weather is unusually chilly? That might be a possibility if getting cold effects how well a baseball bounces. To find out, chill three baseballs. Slip the baseballs into self-sealing plastic bags to keep things clean and leave them in the refrigerator overnight. The next day, perform the same bounce test you did to find the top bouncer. Test again after fifteen minutes and after thirty minutes.

Did you find that being chilled affected how well the balls rebounded? Did they bounce better as they warmed up? According to tests reported in *The Physics of Baseball* (Robert K. Adair, New York: Harper & Row, 1990) a cold ball isn't as elastic as one that's warm. Before a rule was made to stop this practice, the home team supplied balls to the umpire one at a time during a game. And there were rumors that managers sometimes chilled the baseballs that were going to be used when the visiting team was due to bat. Today, all the balls must be given to the umpire two hours before the game—plenty of time for any iced baseballs to warm up.

Inside Puzzle

You may be surprised to learn that a baseball has nearly one-quarter mile of yarn wound around the cork and rubber core. What if you unwound the yarn while circling the bases? How many trips could you make? Clue: 1,760 yards = 1 mile. Check yourself on page 42.

CHAMPION WOMEN ATHLETES

Men aren't the only sports stars. Tackle these problems about women champions. Then check the solution on page 42.

GERTRUDE EDERLE

- Gertrude Ederle was only nineteen when she became the first woman to swim across the English Channel. She also did it in fourteen hours thirty-nine minutes, two hours faster than the record set by a man. At its narrowest point the English Channel is thirty-three kilometers wide. Assuming that Ederle crossed at this point, how many kilometers an hour did she swim?

- In 1985, Libby Riddles became the first woman to win the Alaskan dog sled race. She mushed 1,830 kilometers from Anchorage to Nome, Alaska in three weeks. At that rate, how many kilometers a day did her thirteen-dog team probably cover?

- According to the Guiness Book of Sports Records, 1994 Edition, Galina Chistyakova (Russia) set the current women's long jump record in 1988—24 feet 8 1/4 inches. Olympic competitors are usually able to long jump about five times their body length (height). Based on her long jump record, about how tall would you guess Chistyakova is?

Extra Challenge

Compare your height to how far you can long jump. Check with an adult to be sure where you'll be jumping is a safe place when you try this test. Mark a starting line and jump. Have a friend mark where your feet first land. Measure the distance from the starting line to where you landed. Have your friend also measure your height. Were you able to jump five times your body length? If not, how many times your body length were you able to jump?

Visit the library with a friend, look up biographies of these champion women: Billie Jean King, Martina Navratilova (tennis); Cathy Rigby, Nadia Comaneci (gymnastics), Sonja Henie, Dorothy Hamill (ice skating). Then each make up at least two problems about these women athletes for the other to tackle.

HOW DOES NATURE MEASURE UP?

You'll need to go outdoors to tackle these challenges. Then find the following:

1. The tallest tree within a block of where you live. How tall is it? (You'll need your clinometer to measure this.)

2. Something nearly as long or as wide as your handspan. What did you find? Was it more or less than your handspan? By how much?

3. The flower with the greatest diameter (distance across).

4. Something about the same length as your index finger. What did you find? Was it longer or shorter? By how much?

5. A tree that's close to three meters tall. (Make an estimate and then check your guess with the clinometer.) Was the tree taller or shorter than three meters? By how much?

HERE'S A VINE THAT REALLY MEASURES UP!
Kudzu grows at a rate of 0.3 meters a day to a maximum length of 30 meters.

Measuring Quantities

COOK UP A FORTUNE

If you've ever eaten at a Chinese restaurant, you know part of the fun is finishing the meal with a fortune cookie. Follow the directions below to whip up fortune cookies to share with friends.

You'll need:

1 egg	fork
3 tablespoons of sugar	sheet of clean paper
2 tablespoons margarine	pencil (typewriter or computer if available)
1/4 cup flour	scissors
1/8 teaspoon vanilla extract	oven mitt
1 1/2 teaspoons water	cookie sheet
saucepan	vegetable oil
measuring spoons	sheet of waxed paper
tea cup	spatula
mixing bowl	cooling rack
mixing spoon	

NOTE: *Check that you have permission to use the stove and work carefully. The oven will be hot. You may want to have an adult partner work with you.*

Carefully crack open the egg so the yolk doesn't break. Use an egg separator, if you have one, then pour the egg white into the mixing bowl. Put the yolk in a cup and cover it with clear wrap. Save it in the refrigerator to add to scrambled eggs for breakfast.

Add the sugar to the egg white and whip with a fork. Melt the margarine in the saucepan. Let the margarine cool for about five minutes and then pour it into the egg mixture. Add the flour, vanilla, and water, mixing well. Chill for about thirty minutes.

While you're waiting, cut a dozen strips of paper. Make each about two inches long and a half inch wide. Write short messages in pencil that people can enjoy discovering inside their cookies. Or type the messages first and then cut them out. If you don't have any message ideas, look up horoscopes in the daily newspaper. Then make up similar predictions for the future.

Lightly coat the cookie sheet with vegetable oil and preheat the oven to 350° Fahrenheit. To make one cookie, drop about a teaspoonful of batter on the cookie sheet. Spread it into a circle about three inches in diameter. Be careful to keep the layer of dough thin so it will bake evenly. Form five more cookies. Put the remaining dough back into the refrigerator and put the cookie sheet in the oven. Bake for five minutes or until the edges are golden brown.

Use the oven mitt to move the cookie sheet to the cooling rack. Next, use the spatula to move one cookie to the waxed paper. Be sure your hands are washed and clean. Fold a fortune in half and lay it across the middle of the cookie. Fold the soft, warm cookie in half to cover the fortune. Press the cookie over the edge of the mixing bowl, bending it to a crescent shape. Repeat with each of the other cookies and work quickly. The cookies become stiff and crisp as they cool.

Use the spatula to scrape any remaining crumbs off the cookie sheet. Then do a second batch. If the first cookies don't get crisp as they cool, bake the next batch a little longer.

This recipe makes about a dozen fortune cookies. What operation would you need to perform to figure out how much of each ingredient you'd need to make three dozen cookies? What operation would you need to perform to figure out how much of each ingredient would be needed to make only six cookies? Check yourself on p. 42.

MEASURE UP A TREAT

Want to bake some great cookies? First figure out how much of each ingredient you'll need. Check yourself on page 42. Then follow the baking directions.

You'll need:

   3/4 + 1/4 + 1/4 cups oatmeal

   1/3 + 2/3 cups flour

   Just as much granulated sugar as vegetable oil

   1/2 cup less brown sugar than oatmeal

   1/4 + 1/4 cups raisins

   1/4 + 1/4 teaspoon baking soda

   Half as much vegetable oil as flour

   2 eggs

   Twice as much vanilla as baking soda

NOTE: *Check that you have permission to use the stove and work carefully. The oven will be hot. You may want to have an adult partner work with you.*

Preheat the oven to 350° Fahrenheit. Mix all the ingredients together in a bowl. Lightly grease a cookie sheet with vegetable oil. Spoon out teaspoonful of dough onto the cookie sheet. Bake for twelve minutes or until golden brown. Remove the cookie sheet from the oven with an oven mitt and let cool on a cooling rack. Makes about six dozen.

PUZZLER

Roy had 16 coins totaling $2.45 before he got a hole in his pocket. He lost eight coins totaling $.65. Which of these groups of coins show what he has left? Check yourself on page 43.

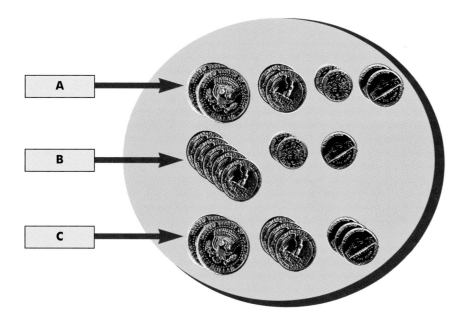

A. Two fifty-cent pieces; two quarters; two dimes; two nickels

B. Five quarters; two dimes; one nickel

C. Two fifty-cent pieces; three quarters; three nickels

MEASURING PUBLIC OPINION

A poll is a way of judging a large group based on a close examination of only part—a sample—of that group. Take a look at the pictograph compiled from the results of a poll that asked, "What's your favorite kind of bread?" Then answer the questions about the poll. Each loaf represents twenty people. Check the solution on page 43.

What's Your Favorite Kind of Bread?

Pita is a middle Eastern round, flat bread that can be opened to form a pocket for a filling. French bread is a long, crusty loaf. Challah is a traditional Jewish bread in the shape of a braid. Pumpernickel is a dark, moist bread. Vanocka is a traditional

Czechoslovakian bread with raisins and almonds. Cha Siu Bon are also known as Chinese steam buns. They are usually served with a meat filling.

1. How many people like French bread?

2. How many more people like pita than cha siu bou?

3. Which bread is more popular, challalh or pumpernickel? How many more people chose this bread?

You may want to look for these breads at your local bakery and sample them yourself. You may also want to read about these and other breads that are popular in different countries.

Extra Challenge

Now conduct a poll of your own.

First, think up a question or choose one of these:

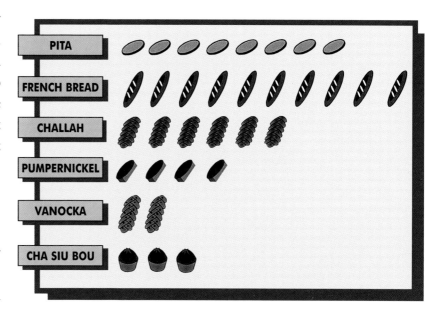

1) What do you do after school or work?

2) Where would you most like to go on vacation?

Next, conduct your poll. Decide in advance how many people you'll ask; the more the better. And be sure your sample reflects all of the group—adults and children, men and women, people who live in apartments and people who live in single-family homes, or whatever. Afterward, record your results on a chart or even better as a pictograph to make them easy to compare. Remember, in a pictograph, each symbol represents a certain number of people in the group polled, so you'll need to decide how many people the symbol will represent.

MEASURING WEIGHTS

MAKE A BALANCE SCALE

While this scale won't give you the weight in grams or ounces, you can measure objects in paper clip units. Use number one standard-size steel paper clips.

To build one you'll need:

2 identical paper cups	tape
1 foot-long ruler	coat hanger (one thin enough to bend easily)
hole punch	
string	2 or 3 heavy books
scissors	table

NOTE: *You may want to have an adult partner work with you.*

First, make a loop of string. Slide it over the ruler, securing it with tape at the six-inch mark. Punch three holes equally spaced around the rim of each cup. Cut six sixteen-inch long strings. Thread one through each hole, tying a knot in the end just below the cup rim. Make the knot big enough that it won't pull through the hole. Bring the three strings for one cup together. Knot them together about three inches from the free ends. Then tie a knot right at the ends to form a loop between the two knots. Slide the string loop over the ruler, anchoring it with tape at the one-inch mark. Tie the strings for the other cup the same way, anchoring the loop at the eleven-inch mark.

Be especially careful to work safely as you bend the coat hanger's hook down so that the whole hook forms a right angle with the rest of the hanger—an angle shaped like the one formed by the wall and ceiling coming together in the corner of a room. Next, lay the hanger flat on the table with the bent hook sticking out over the edge. Or stack up boxes and lay a board on top the way the children did in the picture. Set heavy books on top of the hanger to hold it in place. Slip the scale's center loop over the hanger's hook. After it stops swaying, the ruler should hang level and the two cups should be exactly opposite each other. If the cups don't hang at the same level, adjust the length of the strings. If the ruler isn't level, adjust the string loop or the hanger's hook until it is level.

To weigh an object, put it in one cup. Add paper clips one at a time to the other cup. When the cups are balanced, the number of clips is equal to the object's weight. To find out which of two objects is heavier, simply place one object in each of the cups.

Remember, this scale is only suitable for small, fairly lightweight objects. To weigh large or heavier objects, you could use a kitchen or bathroom scale.

Try It Out

Collect each set of objects listed below. Then hold one object in each hand and decide which you think feels heavier. Put one object of the pair into each of the balance scale cups to check your guess.

1. A dime and two nickels

2. A tea bag and the cap from a two-liter soft drink bottle

3. A button and a penny

Now, arrange all the objects in order from what you believe is the lightest to the heaviest. Weigh each of the objects in paper clip units on the balance scale to see which is really the lightest, next heavier, and so forth. By the way, every two paper clips is equal to about one gram, so you could determine about how many grams each of these items weighs.

MAKE A RUBBER BAND SCALE

This scale will let you quickly and easily compare the weights of small objects.

You'll need:

sturdy wooden or plastic ruler	duct tape
steel paper clip	paper cup
sturdy rubber band	hole punch
crayon	string or yarn

Use duct tape to attach the rubber band to the ruler so it forms a loop starting at zero (0) inches. Be especially careful as you bend the paper clip to form a hook. Slip this hook over the free end of the rubber band. Hold the ruler vertically with the zero end at the top. Make a crayon mark where the bottom of the rubber band loop rests against the ruler.

To weigh something, attach it to the hook. Check how many inches the end of the rubber band loop stretches below the mark you made. The more inches it stretches, the heavier the item.

Because not all items can easily be attached to this hook, you'll also need to make a measuring basket. Punch a hole through the paper cup just below the rim. Punch another hole directly opposite the first one. Thread string or yarn through the holes, tying both ends to form a handle for the cup. Hang the cup on the hook. Make a crayon mark of a different easy-to-see color to show where the end of the rubber band loop rests against the ruler when the measuring basket is attached. Weigh as you did before.

Try It Out

Make a copy of the list below. Use your rubber band scale to weigh each of the following items. Write the number of inches each item made the basket stretch below the mark. Weigh two more items that you find around your house and add these to the list. Then number the items from the lightest (1) to the heaviest (8).

quarter	comb	toothbrush
D-cell flashlight battery	pencil	key

The next time you visit a grocery store, check out what kinds of foods are sold based on their weight and the price per pound. Don't forget to check the meat and dairy departments.

BALANCED ART

Since earliest times, people enjoyed seeing suspended objects move in the breeze. The American artist Alexander Calder, though is credited with being the first to create a mobile, a sculpture designed to move when pushed by air. You can easily create your own mobiles with the help of mathematics.

You'll need:

coat hanger

2 plastic straws

thread or monofilament fishing line

string

balance scale or rubber band scale

scissors

tape

white glue

5 lightweight items (collect items outdoors or make items, such as colorful birds, out of stiff cardboard)

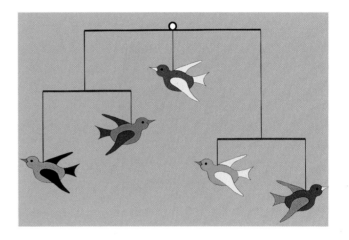

Start from the parts that will hang lowest and work up. The coat hanger is your base. Tie a long piece of string to the hook. Have an adult attach this to a shower rod or in the middle of a doorway where the mobile can swing freely, but you can easily reach the hanger.

Divide the objects into pairs. Use your balance scale or rubber band scale to weigh each item so you'll know which is heavier. Tie a thread to each item—these may be the same length or two different lengths. Tie one item to each end of a straw. Cut a thread fourteen inches long. Tie one end to the hanger and the other end to the straw about two inches from the heavier of the two objects. If the objects are balanced, the straw will hang perfectly horizontal. If the straw slants, slide the thread toward the object at the lower end. Move it only a little at a time, checking after each move until the objects are balanced. Add a dab of glue to anchor the thread on the straw.

Repeat this process to suspend the other pair of objects from the hanger. Make this pair hang at a level that's higher than the first pair. Suspend the final object from the center of the hanger.

WHICH TOILET TISSUE IS STURDIEST WHEN WET?

When the experts at *Consumer Reports* wanted to compare brands of toilet tissue, this was one of the tests they made. You can perform the test yourself. Just follow the steps below and get ready to use your measuring skills.

First, collect three sheets of your family's brand of toilet tissue. Also collect three sheets of at least two other brands of toilet tissue from your friends.

Stretch one sheet of toilet tissue over a small juice glass and secure it with a rubber band. Use a spray bottle, held about five centimeters above the tissue, and spray one squirt of water on it. Drop standard-size steel paper clips—one at a time—from five centimeters above the tissue so they land flat rather than end-first. Continue dropping clips until the tissue breaks. Copy the chart below and record how many paper clip units the tissue was able to support before breaking. Do not count the clip that made the tissue break. Since two paper clips weigh about one gram, divide by two to compute about how many grams the wet tissue supported.

It's important to repeat any test to be sure the results you get aren't just a freak occurrence. So repeat this test with the other two sheets for that brand. Next, add all three totals together and divide by three to find the average grams the wet tissue could support. Then test each of the other brands of toilet tissue to compare.

TOILET TISSUE TEST				
BRAND	**GRAMS SUPPORTED: TEST 1**	**TEST 2**	**TEST 3**	**AVERAGE**

NOTE: *If paper clips aren't available, you can use pennies (about three grams each).*

Think of at least two other tests you could perform to help you decide which toilet tissue is the best buy for your family. Survey your family to find out what features, such as softness, or sturdiness, or cost are most important to them.

WEIGHTY PROBLEMS?

You'll need to put on your thinking cap to solve these puzzles. Here's a strategy that will help you solve these and any story problems:

- Read the problem carefully.

- On scratch paper, list the key facts you'll need to use to solve the problem.

- Work through the math operations you'll need to perform.

- Reread the problem to see if your answer seems logical.

When you think you know the answers, check yourself on page 43.

1. The witch is mixing up a nasty brew. Her recipe calls for twice as many ounces of bat tongue as frog's blood. She'll also need only a fourth as much tail of newt as bat tongue. Most importantly, she'll need four times as much salamander liver oil as bat tongue. The old witch always remembers the number of ounces of bat tongue she needs because it's the same as the number of legs on her pet spider. How much of each ingredient does the old witch need to mix up her brew? (If you aren't sure how many legs a spider has, check an encyclopedia.)

2. Sam, the kennel owner's helper, is supposed to find how much each of the dogs he's caring for weighs. But he can never get Muffy, Spot, or King to stand on the scale alone. Use the following clues to figure out each dog's weight.

Sam, Spot, and Muffy together weigh 241 pounds. Muffy and King together weigh 151 pounds. Sam and King together weigh 315 pounds. Sam by himself weighs 165 pounds.

THE BEANSTALK CAPER

Once upon a time, a young man named Jack sold his cow for three bean seeds that an old man told him were magic beans. His mother thought him a fool, especially since they were very poor and needed money not bean seeds. In a fit of anger, she tossed the seeds out the kitchen window. One seed landed in the garden, and overnight it sprouted. The next morning, Jack and his mother were shocked to discover a huge beanstalk stretching up into the clouds.

Now, if you've ever read this story, you know Jack climbed that beanstalk and discovered a nasty giant's castle. What you may not have heard is that the old man showed up again to warn Jack that the beanstalk would only support 125 pounds before it came crashing down.

Jack wasn't worried climbing up the stalk because he only weighed 75 pounds. But once he got inside the giant's castle, weight became very important because he found several treasures he wanted to carry home. Look at the items listed below. Which do you think Jack should take to get the most value and still be safe climbing down the beanstalk? You'll find some possible solutions on page 43.

(GOOSE LAYS GOLDEN EGGS)
VALUE UNKNOWN
10 POUNDS

(HARP)
$25,000
25 POUNDS

(CROWN)
$10,000
25 POUNDS

(GOLDEN EGGS)
$1,000 EACH
3 POUNDS EACH

(GOLDEN STATUE)
$25,000
70 POUNDS

(MONEY BAGS)
$5,000 EACH
10 POUNDS EACH

(JEWEL CHESTS)
$10,000 EACH
25 POUNDS EACH

(GOLDEN STOOL)
$50,000
50 POUNDS

WEIGH IN

This is a picture of Jessie Tuggle, an Atlanta Falcons linebacker. Before he dresses for the game, Jessie weighs 230 pounds, but he is heavier suited up. Use the picture below to figure out how much his gear weighs. (You'll need to know that there are 16 ounces in a pound.) Now figure out how much Jessie weighs dressed for the game. Check yourself on page 43.

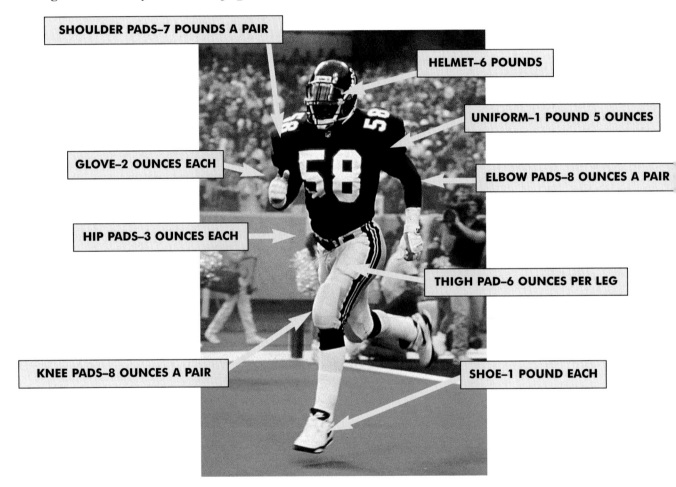

SHOULDER PADS–7 POUNDS A PAIR

HELMET–6 POUNDS

UNIFORM–1 POUND 5 OUNCES

GLOVE–2 OUNCES EACH

ELBOW PADS–8 OUNCES A PAIR

HIP PADS–3 OUNCES EACH

THIGH PAD–6 OUNCES PER LEG

KNEE PADS–8 OUNCES A PAIR

SHOE–1 POUND EACH

Besides his uniform and shoes, a quarterback wears thigh, knee, and shoulder pads. He also zips on a special rib pad that weighs one pound. His helmet is lighter than a linebacker's—it only weighs five pounds. How much less does the quarterback's gear weigh than a linebacker's? Figure it out and then check the solution on page 43.

Now, use the information about a football player's gear to make up two other problems for a friend to solve. And have a friend make up two problems for you to tackle.

MEASURING TEMPERATURES

WEATHER OR NOT

Good morning! It's January 16 and we've got weather information for all you folks about to take a trip. Unfortunately,
we're having a little computer trouble. I'm afraid you'll just
have to use logic to figure out which of the reports is true
and which is false.

CLUE: *Check an atlas to see where these cities are located and
look at the thermometer to get a better idea of what's hot and
what's cool on the Celsius scale.*

Juneau, Alaska: Cloudy and 50° Celsius.
Precipitation expected by late
afternoon.

Miami, Florida: Sunny, clear, with an expected high
today of 25° Celsius.

Detroit, Michigan: Cloudy. Clearing toward midday
with temperatures climbing to 10°
Celsius.

Dallas, Texas: Temperature near 70° Celsius with
precipitation heavy at times.

Did you figure out that the temperatures for Juneau and
Dallas are likely to be false for January? In fact, these
Celsius temperatures would be too hot even for the summer.

What do you think the Celsius temperature is likely to
be outside where you are today? Inside? What strategy did
you use to come to this conclusion? If you have an indoor/
outdoor thermometer available, check your estimate.

MAKE YOUR OWN PRETZELS

This is a recipe where temperature counts. Collect the ingredients listed below. Then follow the steps to cook up a tasty snack.

You'll need:

1/2 cup lukewarm tap water	mixing bowl
1 packet yeast	mixing spoon
1 1/2 cups flour	measuring spoon
1 teaspoon sugar	breadboard
1 egg	cookie sheet
1 teaspoon cool water	oven mitts
coarse kosher salt	cooling rack
vegetable oil	pastry brush (or use clean paper
cooking thermometer	towel rolled up)

NOTE: *Check that you have permission to use the stove and work carefully. You may want to have an adult partner work with you.*

Put the cup of warm water in the bowl. Check the temperature with the cooking thermometer. Granular yeast, the type that comes in a packet, is readily activated by mixing it in water that's about 105° to 115° Fahrenheit. Yeast is alive and won't start to grow if the water it's dissolved in is too cool; if the water's too hot, though, it will kill the yeast.

Mix the sugar and one cup of flour with the dissolved yeast. As the yeast grows, it gives off carbon dioxide gas. This gas is what causes the dough to rise. Work in the remaining flour by hand until it's completely blended. Put the dough on the floured breadboard.

Lightly coat the cookie sheet with vegetable oil. Preheat the oven to 450° Fahrenheit. Beat the egg and one teaspoon of water in the measuring cup. Divide the dough into pieces about two by four inches. Roll one dough section between your hands until it forms a rope about fifteen inches long. Place it on the cookie sheet, crossing the two ends over the middle section. Supposedly, the monks who created pretzels meant the crossed sections to represent arms crossed in prayer.

Use the pastry brush to brush each pretzel with the egg mixture. Sprinkle with salt. Bake for ten minutes or until golden brown. Use the oven mitts and be careful when you lift the pan out of the oven. Let the pretzels cool before eating.

HOW DO YOU KEEP A CUP OF HOT TEA HOT?

Do you like to drink hot tea? Would you like to find a way to keep your cup of tea hot after it's poured? First, follow the steps to brew a pot of tea. Then follow the investigation guide to develop and test a strategy for keeping your tea hot.

According to expert tea taster William Hall at the Charleston Tea Plantation on Wadmalaw Island, South Carolina, the following steps should be followed to brew the perfect pot of tea:

1. Plan on about eight ounces of water for each cup of tea you want to serve. If you don't know how many ounces your teapot holds, fill it full of cold tap water—one cup at a time. One cup equals eight ounces. Measure out one teaspoon of tea leaves for each cup of tea.

2. Fill a teakettle, bring to a boil, and fill the teapot to preheat it. Next, dump out the remaining hot water and refill the teakettle with fresh, cold tap water. It's best to start with fresh, cold water because it has more oxygen than warm water and oxygen helps enhance the flavor of the tea.

3. As soon as the kettle boils a second time, empty the teapot. Put in the tea and fill the teapot with boiling water. After the tea leaves are picked, they are dried. This makes the leaves curl, sealing in the tea's natural juices. A burst of boiling water is needed to make the leaves open to release the flavorful juices.

4. Put the lid on the teapot and let the tea brew for three to six minutes. Then stir once, wait a few minutes for the tea leaves to settle, and serve.

Now that you've made perfect hot tea, how can you keep the tea from cooling off? Would it help to wrap cotton cloth around the cup? Would wool or paper be a better insulator? What if you put a lid on top of the cup? The following guide will help you develop an idea and test it.

Developing Your Strategy

Brainstorm. Make a list of all the things you could do to keep your cup of tea from cooling off. Allow yourself ten minutes for brainstorming. Then evaluate your list of ideas, thinking about which is the most likely to be successful. No fair reheating your tea on the stove or in a microwave oven.

NOTE: *Check your idea with an adult to be sure what you've planned will be safe for you to try.*

Challenge Time

Prepare a pot of tea. Collect two candy thermometers and two identical teacups. You'll also need whatever materials are called for by your plan.

Pour exactly the same amount of tea into each of the two teacups. Immediately take the temperature of each cup and record this information. Now, put your strategy into action on just one of the cups. The other cup of tea will be your control. A control lets you compare your test results to what will normally happen. Check and record the temperature of the tea after five minutes and again after ten and fifteen minutes. How well did your strategy work? Based on what you discovered, how might you modify your tea warmer so it will work even better?

This may look like a field full of ordinary shrubbery, but it isn't. The leaves of these special bushes are used to make tea.

MEASURING VOLUME

BOTTLED WATER

Wondering how to measure something, such as a bottle, that isn't flat? The answer is to measure how much it can hold. That measurement is called *volume*. Sometimes, though, a container's shape can make it appear to hold more or less than it really does. See for yourself.

You'll need:

at least 5 different clear containers

measuring cup

blue and red marking pens

food coloring

Color water to make it easier to see. Pour eight ounces of water into the largest container. (One cup equals eight ounces.) Use the blue pen to mark the water level on the side of the container. Do you think the container will hold at least eight more ounces? If so, make a red mark where you think the next eight-ounce level will be. Check yourself by pouring eight more ounces of water into the container. How close was your estimate? Based on what you have seen the bottle hold, estimate how many more ounces you think will be needed to completely fill the bottle. Test your prediction by filling the bottle.

Now, repeat these steps to measure how much each of the other bottles will hold. Does experience make you a better judge? Did any one bottle fool you? Why do you think it was difficult to predict how much water that bottle would hold?

Go on a bottle hunt at your local grocery store. Find at least two different bottles that say they contain the same amount. Try to find two very different bottles, such as one that is tall and skinny and one that is short and fat. What's in each of the two bottles? Why do you suppose the manufacturers chose to make their bottle this shape?

WHICH IS THE BETTER BUY?

You can use volume to discover how much more you actually get when you buy the large soft drink rather than the small size. This will help you decide which is really the better buy—the large or the small.

To find out, you'll need to get one large and one small soft drink cup from a local fast-food restaurant. First, fill the small cup with water to within an inch of the top—about as full as it would be if you purchased it. Pour this water into the large cup and mark the level on the side. How much of the large cup did this fill: one-third, half, more?

Now that you've seen roughly how much more you get when you buy a large drink, find out exactly. Empty the water from the small cup into a measuring cup that has ounce measurements on it. Figure out how many ounces of drink were in the small cup.

Next, fill the large cup within an inch of the top and measure the amount of water it holds.

How much more liquid do you get when you purchase the large drink? If the large drink costs $1.28 and the small drink costs $.96, what strategy will you need to use to figure out which is the better buy? Check yourself on page 43.

How do you suppose adding ice to a soft drink affects the amount of liquid you get in a small and a large drink? Plan and perform an investigation to test your idea. Check the costs of large and small drinks at several different fast food restaurants in your area. Which is the better buy at each—the large or the small soft drink?

WHAT'S GOING DOWN THE DRAIN?

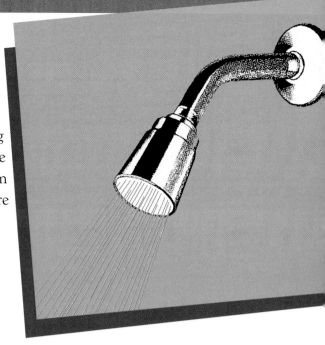

Did you ever wonder how much water is going down the drain while you shower? Does it make a big difference if the water flow is low, medium or fast? One way you can find out is to measure the volume of water going down the drain.

You'll need:

2 large plastic buckets or wastebaskets

waterproof watch with a second hand or windup kitchen timer

empty 1-liter plastic soft drink bottle

plastic cup

NOTE: *Use a container to store water collected during test so the water won't be wasted, use it to water plants or wash a pet.*

To start the test, turn the cold water shower tap on low. Position a bucket so it catches the falling water. After thirty seconds, shut off the water. Bail out what you collected by filling the liter bottle and then emptying it into another bucket. Write down how many full liters of water you collected and any fraction of a liter more. Multiply by two to find out how much water would have been collected in sixty seconds—one whole minute. Repeat this test two more times. Add together your three totals and divide by three to learn the average amount of low water flow in one minute. Compute the medium and fast level flows the same way.

The next time you take a shower, decide what water flow level you'll use. Then time your shower. While you're scrubbing, decide what operation you'll need to use to find out how much water is going down the drain while you're cleaning up. When you think you know, read on.

To find out how much water goes down the drain while you're showering, multiply what's lost in one minute at that flow rate times the number of minutes you showered. Now, ask the other members of your family to select a water flow level and time their showers. Use this information to compute how much water is lost as each family member showers.

Fresh water is an important resource that needs to be preserved. Hold a family meeting. Discuss ways your family could use less water while showering.

JUST THE RIGHT TOOL

Which of the measuring tools would you need to use in each of the following situations?

Measuring tape   *Thermometer*   *Measuring cup*   *Scale*

Check the solutions on page 43.

1. Adding milk to the cake mix.

2. Determining how much to pay for three apples that are $.69 a pound.

3. Setting up the bases for a baseball diamond.

4. Checking the turkey to see if the interior of the bird is cooked.

5. Seeing how much you've grown since last year.

6. Deciding whether or not to wear a coat when you go outdoors.

7. Adding water to make jello.

8. Putting the right amount of postage on a letter.

9. Finding out how far the paper airplane flew.

10. Deciding how long the new window curtains should be.

THE END?—NEVER!

Now you've discovered that measuring is fun, and you have some new tools to help you measure. What's more, you've learned that measuring can help you tackle problems and make decisions. So even though this is the end of the book, there's lots of action ahead. Be curious, and it won't be long before you're measuring again.

STILL MORE CHALLENGES

Here are still more activities to keep you measuring.

1. Find out if what you think is a shortcut home really is shorter. First, use your hodometer to find out how many meters it is to your destination on the regular route. Then plan how you will go home along a shortcut. Be sure and check with an adult that this route is safe for you. Then go home along your shortcut, measuring the distance with your hodometer. Were you surprised by the results?

2. Just for fun, go to a baseball diamond in your neighborhood. Measure the distance between the bases with the hodometer to be sure it really is ninety feet—the distance between bases on an official baseball diamond. Have someone time how fast you can run the bases. The record is held by Ernest Evar Swanson who took only 13.3 seconds to circle the bases at the stadium in Columbus, Ohio, in 1932. How much faster or slower were you?

3. What is the tallest tree you can find growing in your neighborhood? What is the shortest tree? Check *The Guiness Book of Records* for the world's tallest and shortest trees. How do your neighborhood champs compare?

4. Here's another pattern for making a mobile. Use what you learned in Balanced Art (p. 25) to make this style of mobile.

SOLUTIONS

p.4 • Wild Bugs

Checkered beetle 1/4 inch; Strawberry clearwing moth 1 1/2 inch; Cuckoo wasp 1/4 inch; Texas beetle larva 1/2 inch; Pink cricket 2 inches

p.6 • Eye Tricks

Red and blue line are equal; height of hat and width of hat brim are equal; both center circles are the same size.

p.11 • Manute Slept Here

To see how much of Manute will hang over each bed, you could first change his height into inches: 7 feet x 12 inches in one foot + 7 inches= 91 inches. Then subtract to see how much longer Manute is than each bed's length and diagonal measurement. He'll hang over in a twin bed (17 inches lengthwise or 10 inches if he stretches out diagonally) and a full-sized bed (17 inches lengthwise and 3 inches on the diagonal). Manute could be comfortable, though, in either a queen-size or king-size bed if he's willing to sleep on the diagonal. He'll have 5 inches to spare in a queen size bed and 17 inches in a king.

p.12 • Running Home

It's 90 feet between each base. One way to find out how many feet Hank Aaron had to run to complete one home run is to multiply 90 by 4; the result is 360 feet. Divide this total by 3, the number of feet in one yard, to discover the total for one home run—120 yards. Multiply 755, the number of runs Hank Aaron hit, by 120 to compute the total number of yards he ran—90,600 yards. Since that number is larger than 16,726 yards, Payton's rushing record, subtract 16,726 from 90,600, to find out how much farther Aaron ran for his career record—73,874 yards farther.

p.14 • Inside Puzzle

The baseball's yarn would let you circle the bases 3.67 times while it was unwinding.

p.15 • Champion Women Athletes

- Gertrude Ederle swam about 2.25 kilometers per hour. Multiply 14 times 60 to get the number of minutes in 14 hours (840). Add 39 to get the total minutes (879). Divide by 60 to get the time as hours (14.65). Divide 33 kilometers by 14.65 to get the average (2.25 kilometers per hour).
- Libby Riddles' team averaged 87.14 kilometers a day during their race. (1830 kilometers divided by 21 days of racing.)
- Galina Chistyakova is about 5 feet tall (Round 24 feet 8 1/4 inches to 25 feet and divide by 5.)

p.17 • Cook Up A Fortune

You would need to multiply each ingredient amount by three to bake three dozen cookies. You would need to divide the amount of each ingredient in half to make six fortune cookies.

p.19 • Measure Up A Treat

1 1/4 cups oatmeal	1/2 cup raisins
1 cup flour	1/2 teaspoon baking soda
1/2 cup granulated sugar	1/2 cup vegetable oil
3/4 cup brown sugar	2 eggs
1 teaspoon vanilla	

p.20 • Puzzler
A. Roy still has two fifty-cent pieces, two quarters, two dimes, two nickels.

p.19 • Measuring Public Opinion
1. How many people like French bread? 200
2. How many more people like pita than cha siu bou? 100
3. Which bread is more popular, challah or pumpernickel? Challah—forty more people prefer it.

p.28 • Weighty Problems
1. All spiders have 8 legs. So the old witch needs 8 ounces of bat tongue, 4 ounces of frog blood, 2 ounces of tail of newt, and 32 ounces of salamander liver oil.
2. Since you know Sam weighs 165 pounds, you can subtract his weight from 315 to learn that King weighs 150 pounds. Then you can subtract King's weight to discover that Muffy only weighs one pound. Subtracting, Muffy's and Sam's combined weights reveals that Spot weighs 75 pounds.

p.29 • The Beanstalk Caper
While you'll probably think of other possibilities, here are two. Jack could just carry away the golden stool for a fast $50,000. Or to take a chance on a longer investment, he might take one chest, one bag, one egg, and the goose. He'd still be two pounds lighter than the weight the bean stalk can support. And while he'd only have gotten away with a present value of $16,000, the goose might continue laying $1,000 eggs every day or so for a number of years.

p.30 • Weigh In
A linebacker's gear weighs about eighteen pounds, eleven ounces. If that doesn't sound like much, pack your book bag so it weighs nineteen pounds. Now, run with it. Suited up, Jessie and his equipment weigh 248 pounds 11 ounces.

The quarterback's gear only weighs about seventeen pounds ten ounces—about one pound one ounce less than the linebacker's gear.

p.38 • Which is the Better Buy?
In most fast food restaurants, a small cup holds 12 ounces and the large holds 32 ounces. To find out whether the large or small size soft drink is the better buy, you had to first find the cost per ounce for each cup size. To compute the cost per ounce for the small drink, divide the price by the number of ounces that cup usually holds. Do the same for the large drink. In this example, when you divide $.96 by 12 ounces, the price is 8 cents per ounce. When you divide $1.28 by 32 ounces, the price is 4 cents per ounce.

p.40 • Just the Right Tool
1. Measuring cup
2. Scale
3. Measuring tape
4. Thermometer
5. Measuring tape
6. Thermometer
7. Measuring cup
8. Scale
9. Measuring tape
10. Measuring tape

Index